Lingo Dingo
and the
Ukrainian chef

Written by Mark Pallis
Illustrated by James Cottell

For my awesome sons Oscar and Felix - MP

For Leo and Juniper - JC

LINGO DINGO AND THE UKRAINIAN CHEF

All rights reserved. This book or any portion thereof may not be reproduced or used in any manner whatsoever without the express written permission of the publisher except for the use of brief excerpts in a review.

Story edited by Natascha Biebow, Blue Elephant Storyshaping
First Printing, 2022
ISBN: 978-1-915337-11-5
NeuWestendPress.com

Lingo Dingo
and the
Ukrainian chef

Written by Mark Pallis
Illustrated by James Cottell

NEU WESTEND PRESS

This is Lingo. She's a Dingo and she loves helping.
Anyone. Anytime. Anyhow.

Lingo often helps her stylish neighbour Gunther, who lives by himself next door. She does a few jobs and has a nice chat. It makes Gunther feel good and it makes Lingo feel good too.

One day, Lingo arranged a special birthday party for Gunther. She even ordered a cake from a famous Ukrainian chef.

There was a knock at the door, "It must be the cake!" said Lingo. But it was a monkey.

"Привіт. Мене звуть Шеф Ноно. У мене проблема," he said.

Oh no. I can't speak Ukrainian yet, thought Lingo. *Maybe 'Привіт' is like 'Hello'.*

Привіт = Hello; **Мене звуть** = My name is;
У мене проблема = I have a problem.

"Привіт," said Lingo. Chef Nono replied slowly,
Vybach. YA ne mozhu spekty tort do dnya narodzhennya
"Вибач. Я не можу спекти торт до дня народження."

"I don't understand," said Lingo. "But let me guess. You want…"

Вибач = I am sorry; **торт до дня народження** = birthday cake
Я не можу спекти торт до дня народження = I cannot make the birthday cake

A trolley?

Vizok? Ni
Візок? Ні.

A gherkin?

Kornishon? Ni
Корнішон? Ні.

Balloons?

Povitryani kul'ky? Ni.
Повітряні кульки? Ні.

Візок = a trolley; **Корнішон** = a gherkin;
Повітряні кульки = balloons; **Ні** = no

Chef Nono and Lingo whizzed around the kitchen:

Os′ tobi fartukh
Ось тобі фартух.

Vinchyk
Вінчик.

Myska dlya zmishuvannya
Миска для змішування.

фартух = apron; **Ось тобі** = for you; **Вінчик** = a whisk
Миска для змішування = a mixing bowl

Pereday meni maslo, tsukor
"Передай мені масло, цукор,
yaytsya ta boroshno, bud☐ laska
яйця та борошно, будь ласка," said Chef.

Lingo wasn't sure what those words meant, so she just grabbed fish, coffee and onions instead.

Ryba, kava ta tsybulya
"Риба, кава та цибуля.
Gidota
Гидота!" laughed Chef.

Передай мені = pass me; **масло** = butter; **цукор** = sugar; **яйця** = eggs; **та** = and; **борошно** = flour; **будь ласка** = please; **Риба** = fish; **кава** = coffee; **цибуля** = onions; **Гидота** = disgusting

Chef plopped butter, sugar, eggs and flour into a bowl. "So that's what 'масло, цукор, яйця та борошно' means!" laughed Lingo.

maslo, tsukor, yaytsya ta boroshno

"Я змішую, ти змішуєш, ми змішуємо," said Chef and together they began to mix the cake.

YA zmishuyu, ty zmishuyesh, my zmishuyemo

Я змішую = I mix; **ти змішуєш** = you mix; **ми змішуємо** = we mix

"Нарешті, розпушувач. Дві ложки," said Chef. Lingo guessed 'розпушувач' meant baking powder, but how much?

Before she could ask, Chef hurried away, saying, "Вибач, мені потрібно зробити пі-пі."

Lingo laughed, "I can guess what 'пі-пі' means!"

Нарешті = finally; розпушувач = baking powder; Дві = two; ложки = spoonfulls; Вибач = excuse me; мені потрібно зробити пі-пі = I need to do a wee wee

I wonder if this is too much? thought Lingo as she added ten spoonfulls of 'розпушувач' to the mix.

She carefully put everything into the oven and before long, a sweet cakey smell filled the kitchen.

розпушувач = baking powder

Shcho trapylosya? Vono velychezne
"Що трапилося? Воно величезне!" said Chef.

Lingo realised she had added too much baking powder.
"Sorry," she said sheepishly.

Що трапилося = what happened; **Воно величезне** = it is huge

They somehow got the cake out of the oven but ...

it was so big ...

... they couldn't hold it. "Disaster!" cried Lingo. "Катастрофа!" wailed Chef.

Katastrofa

Катастрофа = disaster

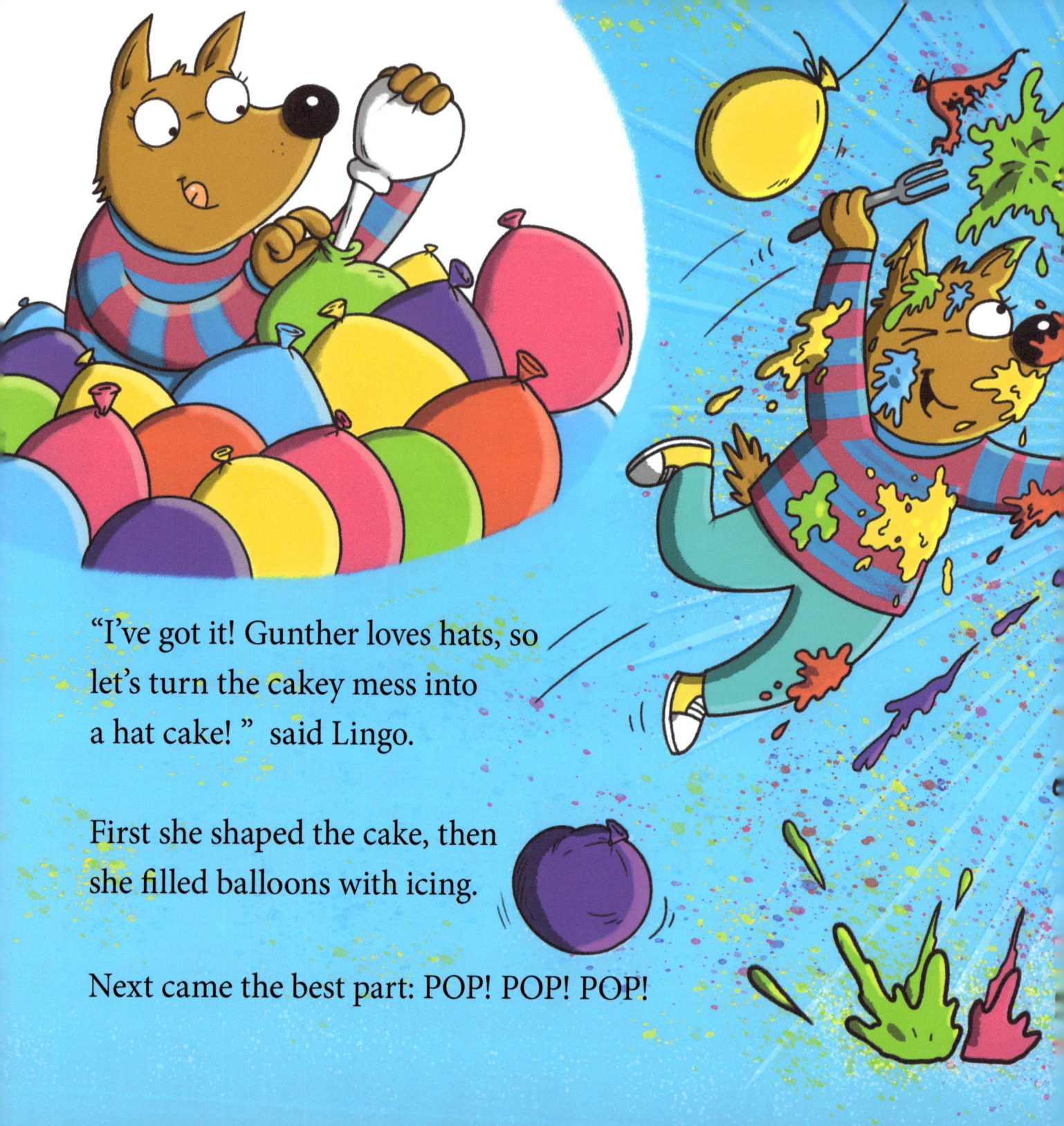

"I've got it! Gunther loves hats, so let's turn the cakey mess into a hat cake!" said Lingo.

First she shaped the cake, then she filled balloons with icing.

Next came the best part: POP! POP! POP!

It was a messy job but in the end, the cake looked fantastic. "Червоний, помаранчевий, жовтий, зелений, синій. Фантастика!" said Chef.
Chervonyy, pomaranchevyy, zhovtyy, zelenyy, syniy. Fantastyka

Червоний = red; **помаранчевий** = orange; **жовтий** = yellow;
зелений = green; **синій** = blue; **Фантастика** = fantastic

There was a knock at the door.
"Двері!" said Chef.
_{Dveri}

It was Gunther, and he was wearing his special hat!

"Thank you. This makes me feel so special," said Gunther. "You are special," replied Lingo.

Двері = door

Gunter was thrilled with his cake.
Chef's deep voice sang "З Днем народження тебе..."

Z Dnem narodzhennya tebe...

З Днем народження тебе = Happy birthday to you

Dmukhai
"Дмухай!" said Chef.

Gunther blew out all the candles in one puff and everyone tucked in.

Дмухай = blow

YA yim, ty yisy, vin yist′, vona yist′, vony yidyat′
"Я їм, ти їси, він їсть, вона їсть, вони їдять," laughed Chef.
"my yimo
ми їмо!" added Lingo proudly.

Я їм = I eat; **ти їси** = you eat; **він їсть** = he eats;
вона їсть = she eats; **вони їдять** = they eat; **ми їмо** = we eat

Everyone was happy.
<small>YA shchaslyvyy</small>
"Я щасливий,
<small>ty shchaslyva</small>
ти щаслива.
<small>My vsi shchaslyvi</small>
Ми всі щасливі," said Chef.

Я щасливий = I am happy; **ти щаслива** = you are happy;
Ми всі щасливі = we are all happy;

Baking a cake, helping a friend, learning a new language... what a day!

But now it was time for bed. It was time to dream about all the fun things that might happen tomorrow.

Learning to love languages

An additional language opens a child's mind, broadens their horizons and enriches their emotional life. Research has shown that the time between a child's birth and their sixth or seventh birthday is a "golden period" when they are most receptive to new languages. This is because they have an in-built ability to distinguish the sounds they hear and make sense of them. The Story-powered Language Learning Method taps into these natural abilities.

How the Story-powered language learning Method works

We create an emotionally engaging and funny story for children and adults to enjoy together, just like any other picture book. Studies show that social interaction, like enjoying a book together, is critical in language learning.

Through the story, we introduce a relatable character who speaks only in the new language. This helps build empathy and a positive attitude towards people who speak different languages. These are both important aspects in laying the foundations for lasting language acquisition in a child's life.

As the story progresses, the child naturally works with the characters to discover the meanings of a wide range of fun new words. Strategic use of humour ensures that this subconscious learning is rewarded with laughter; the child feels good and the first seeds of a lifelong love of languages are sown.

For more information and free learning resources visit www.neuwestendpress.com

You can learn more words and phrases with these hilarious, heartwarming stories from NEU WESTEND PRESS

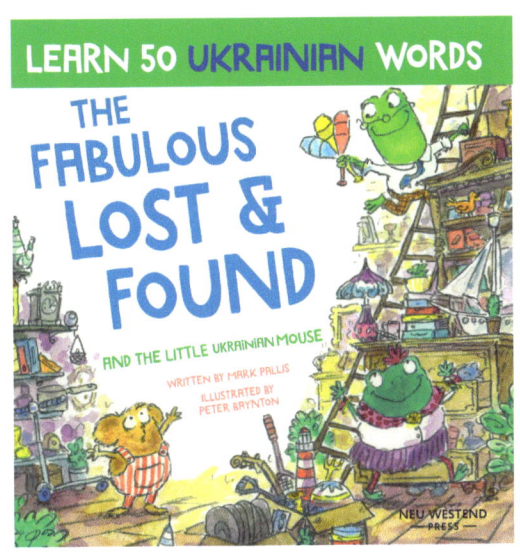
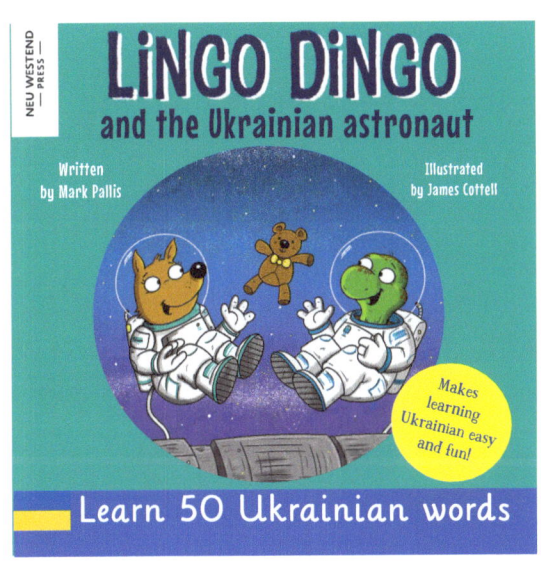

@MARK_PALLIS on twitter
www.neuwestendpress.com

To download your FREE certifcate, and more cool stuff, visit
www.neuwestendpress.com

@jamescottell on INSTAGRAM
www.jamescottellstudios.co.uk

"I want people to be so busy laughing, they don't realise they're learning!"
Mark Pallis

Crab and Whale is the bestselling story of how a little Crab helps a big Whale. It's carefully designed to help even the most energetic children find a moment of calm and focus. It also includes a special mindful breathing exercise and affirmation for children.

Featured as one of Mindful.org's 'Seven Mindful Children's books'

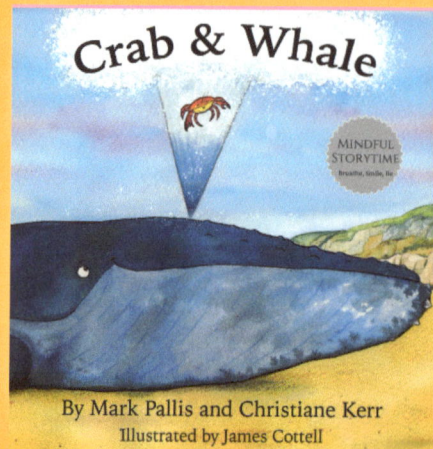

Do you call them hugs or cuddles?

In this funny, heartwarming story, you will laugh out loud as two loveable gibbons try to figure out if a hug is better than a cuddle and, in the process, learn how to get along.

A perfect story for anyone who loves a hug (or a cuddle!)

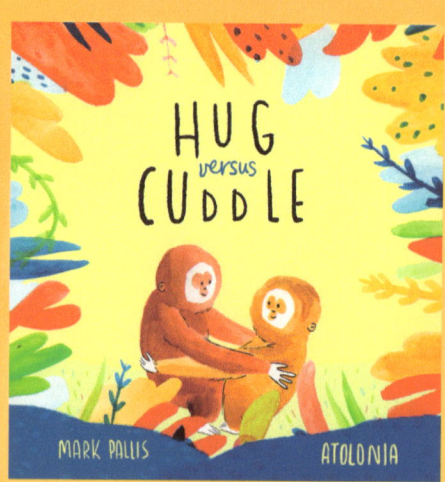

www.markpallis.com

www.ingramcontent.com/pod-product-compliance
Lightning Source LLC
Chambersburg PA
CBHW040021130526
44590CB00036B/46